I Have Something to Say: The Road to Transparency

Kezia M.K. Hodge

BK Royston Publishing
P. O. Box 4321
Jeffersonville, IN 47131
502-802-5385
http://www.bkroystonpublishing.com
bkroystonpublishing@gmail.com

Cover Design:
Book Photography: Childhood Picture: Sharon Hodge
Adult Picture: Nicki Watkins
Back Cover Photo: Courtney Miller

ISBN-13: 978-1-951941-96-3

Printed in the United States of America

Dedication

I want to dedicate this to my entire village, specifically my daughter, Kirsten and cousin, Shivawn.

.

Acknowledgements

I have to begin by thanking God for his perfect timing.

To my family...mom, dad, James, Lisa, Phil, and Kenya for their constant prayers, encouragement, and belief in me. I assuredly would not be here today without your UNCONDITIONAL love. I love you.

A special thanks to my soul sisters Dianna, Cassie, and Amber who've had nothing but positive affirmations since I began this project. Our connection keeps me afloat. It's hard to believe we haven't been friends our entire lives.

Dawne and Autra who God led me to share this with in the early stages, your feedback helped me to know this is something I had to move forward with, thank you.

And finally to Jermelle, my rider who has been there to see the highs, lows, tears, triumphs and knows where all of the skeletons are buried ha! You are invaluable to my life. Words will never do justice to the friendship and sisterhood we share.

Table of Contents

Foreword

Kirsten and I basically grew up together. When I was the age she is now I had already been a mom for four years. While I was dedicated to being the best mom I possibly could, I still felt like my dreams were attainable at the same time. As life went on, my focus became more about her—which wasn't a bad thing—but somewhere along the way what I wanted in life became less important. Once she graduated from college and settled into a career, the inspiration she had always been to me was magnified. Her attitude is so no nonsense. If she wants it, she makes a plan to do it and failure, as cliché as it sounds, is just not an option. She and her friends constantly motivate each other, support one another, and use positivity to build the other. When she recently revived her love of dance after leaving it briefly behind to secure a stable living, it was as if she'd given me permission to dream again. Thank you, mi hija. I love you immensely.

Growing up, our family didn't do the big reunions that most do. We saw each other once or twice a year because of distance, but those times were priceless. However, when social media became a thing, you were able to connect daily with family that normally you'd have to write to or make a phone call to check on. Reading about my cousin Shivawn's life and learning who she was as an adult made me happy but sad that we hadn't grown up closer because I can guarantee we would have been best friends. When she wrote a book, I was so proud. I would share it different places though I had never read it. Each time it'd actually crossed my mind to purchase it, I — of course — had no money. Then I hit a hard patch in life and she reached out for my address because she wanted to send me a copy. I am all about timing because don't you know it was over a year before she actually did. I started reading it the day I got it. I also stopped reading it that same day...you know life. I found it under some things about a week later and put it on my nightstand. I didn't know why, but I knew it was going to be the key to me finally completing what I'd started. She frequently uses the word "storyteller." It wasn't until I was almost done with this project that I understood that's exactly what I am...a storyteller.

March 9, 2019, she sent me a message saying, "I hope one day you feel empowered enough to tell your story. Whatever it looks like." That day is today, and I thank her for that.

I don't claim to be a writer. To be completely honest, I'm not one who typically enjoys sitting down to read a good book. It was through events over the last few years that I found relief when I would write out what I was feeling. Not in a journal per se, but when something was eating at me, when I couldn't let go of a thought be it positive or negative, I would just begin to write down everything that was going on in my head until I was able to breathe a sigh of relief. I did this on social media, and that’s where I found an audience who not only listened but also encouraged me, related to me, and learned from and with me.

My life, in My Words

As I sit here typing, still in the towel I wrapped around myself leaving the bathroom, I had to laugh. I went to get my laptop; it was dead. Went and got the charger, but the outlets in my room are two pronged. Unplugged everything in my son's room to take his three-prong outlet, and then I began. I create and plan in my head all day long pretty much every day. When I get home from picking up my son, make dinner, check homework, and make sure we've showered, those ideas always find their final resting place still there in my mind. Sleep beckons...maybe tomorrow, which turns into next week, next month, and, well, you get the picture.

Kobe Bryant died today. I tried to pull myself off of Twitter, Facebook, Instagram, but the stories kept me glued to my screen for far too long. I couldn't believe the tragedy that had befallen this family, him, a man exactly my age who when he got up like most of us this morning, gave no thought to the fact that he might not make it back home to his loved ones. I finally put my phone down and headed to the shower after telling my

Fb friends and family to live each day as if it were their last and that I loved them. I made a vow to start writing tomorrow. Under the falling water, I decided it had to be tonight, no more excuses.

Here's the thing I've known for a while: that I wanted to write a book about my son and his escapades, which I actually started probably a good year ago and never finished. At some point I knew what I wrote first had to be about me, my life, and my journey, which I'm sure is like so many others. It's not that I'm this ultra-interesting person, but there is just so much I want and need to say.

I found my voice, funny enough, on social media when I began being completely honest about how I felt about things going on in and around my life. People kept saying, “you should write a book about your son.” As I said, it’s in the works, but not done. A lady in my church told me that I was a good storyteller. Another person said, “the movies really need your talent.” Then it dawned on me that, yes, many of my posts were about my unique child but what it came down to was how I conveyed not only his stories, but my own, my daughter's, and my family's, and friends'. I shared things that let others know they weren't alone in their thinking. The support I'd get even from social media lurkers at times made me know people were actually listening to what I had to say, and not only that, they valued it. All that being said, I don't know what this book will be about:, I just knew I had to start writing because I have things I want to share with the world, with you.

Social media has been a blessing and a curse for me, a trigger of sorts. It has also forced me to face things that honestly I never knew were wrong. Let's just start with the whole R. Kelly debacle. Love him or hate him, you are kidding yourself if you believe he didn't do anything wrong. I was furious that we were so publicly telling young black girls and women hey we don't believe you; you knew what you were doing; stop being fast. I posted a meme a while back that said, "Ain't no teenage girl fast enough to catch a grown man that ain't attracted to children." So when people started blaming everyone but him, including friends and people I'd grown to respect, I began to think of my own experience.

Though he wasn't as old as R. Kelly, he was old enough to know better. When I was 12, maybe 13, my innocence would cease to exist. You see, when you go through trauma some things stay vivid while other memories are vague, even ones people not in the situation can't believe you don't remember. What I do remember is that I was wearing a green and white stripped sun dress with a pocket on the front. Thinking back, I'm not sure where my friend was or why I would have stayed at her house if she wasn't there, in any case I found myself on the stairs that day with her brother, who was in high school.

He kissed me and I remember feeling like, "wow this older guy likes me?"

Things progressed, and before I knew it, my virginity was a thing of the past. I never said, "stop." I never said anything. I just lay there. I don't know that I knew I had the option of saying, "this is not OK." I can't recall what happened when it was over. The next memory I have is telling one of the high school girls at my church what happened and from there it got back to my parents somehow. I'd find out years later that my mom and someone else had to physically hold my dad back from going after the guy. I'd also find out details I'd blocked out after letting my mom read my first draft of this.

She told me it happened in July of 1990, and I had just turned 12 in the spring. He was a few months shy of 18 and for that reason could not be prosecuted. She said in September we were lying across her bed when I told her myself what had happened. My friend had been downstairs the whole time. When it was over and tears streamed down my face, he'd asked if I was OK. Then, as if nothing had happened, I walked to the store with my friend. My mom talked about being thankful that I had actually told two young girls in our church but sad that I had been carrying that burden around for two months. Back then I couldn't understand why everyone was so up in arms about it. Now that I am a parent, and have worked with children for over 20 years, I know exactly where the anger stemmed from. We have to advocate for our children, even when we feel like they're acting "grown." They are in fact NOT grown.

Life went on for me and it wasn't until I was in my 40's that it hit me that many of my life choices over the years were directly connected to what happened and what I'd lost that day. I would go on to become more sexually active than any young person should ever be, with the follow up to my virginity being taken coming mere weeks later. On a summer field trip at a pool, we were all just lounging around. I was floating in a tube when suddenly my legs were being pulled around the waist of one of my childhood friends. Again why didn't I say anything? Why did he think this was OK? Then it happened, an intimate encounter in a very public setting that I had not asked for and with a voice that did not know how to say stop. Honestly, from then on sex was the furthest thing from my mind, but I did it because, well, it's what he, whoever he was, at the time wanted. This went on through high school; then I found myself pregnant and headed to college. It was time for me to grow up. I had more than myself to think about.

I went on to school, focused on my education, and somehow found myself in love. He obviously knew I was with child considering the large appendage hanging from the front side of my body. Yet here, we were a girl from the country and boy from the city figuring this thing called love and life out. Things were good; for a long time things were good. Sure, we broke up and got back together a million times in between, but this was my person; he was going to be my forever.

My daughter was his daughter; his stink bink. We were happy. Then my world came crashing down. We were on a break once again so I remember being annoyed when he called to wish my baby a happy fifth birthday a day early. He left a message, which I erased right after playing it. The next morning while preparing for her birthday party, my parents called to tell me I should get there a little early. I didn't. So standing in this very public venue, surrounded by gifts and cake, my dad tells me my forever is gone. He'd died in a car crash early that morning. All I remember of that day is backing away from my dad, screaming that it couldn't be true; he'd just called last night. But it was true, and things wouldn't be any kind of normal for an extremely long time after that day.

Convinced I'd never experience what we'd had again, slowly I sank back into accepting "love" that clearly wasn't love. Then at some point I said, "I'm going to own my sexuality and I became the aggressor." I got to them before they could talk me into something I didn't want. This only left me empty when all was said and done. All the while I'm raising an impressionable little girl. My girl…we were literally growing up together. She was born into college life. My idea of being responsible at that time was waiting until she was gone on the weekend to drink and party. Also not having a "friend" over until she was asleep. What in the world was I doing?

During these years, there were a few who came close to being "the one," but neither the timing nor my mindset was ever quite right. I went on to graduate and move back home briefly before making the move to Atlanta. It was time to pull it together and pursue my dreams of singing professionally. If I didn't go for it now, I probably never would. With the move came new struggles. Though my oldest brother lived in the area, he was a good hour drive away. It seemed like all I did was work and come home. I never really made any friends, and everything was super expensive! Once I found a church home, I joined the choir, got my daughter heavily involved in their children's program, and became a model member.

Still the reason I'd come there was evading me, especially when there were times I didn't even know where our next meal was going to come from. Sure, I could have reached out to family but I wanted to do this on my own, so while I made sure my daughter never went without eating there were several nights I went to bed hungry. Eventually, I fell behind on rent and one day came home to an eviction notice on our door. I ended up borrowing money from my employer, who subsequently began making our work environment a living hell.

Once I'd paid it back, I moved on to another job and a new apartment. Things were going pretty well. We'd been home

(Louisville) to see my parents for Easter, I believe, and I'd later find out about the secret meeting that occurred between my daughter and her granny. My birthday was a few weeks later and she said, "Mom I'm taking you to that restaurant you've been wanting to try." I'm sure I laughed, and then she pulled out the $100 my mom had given her to hide from me. She'd warned her not to give it to me because I'd spend it on bills and she was right. I vaguely remember the food, not the best, but the memory of that moment still makes me tear up even as I write this today.

Anyway, I finished up my first year at my new job, and then my boss called me in to talk with me. As she spoke about my performance, it dawned on me that I was being fired. The things she was saying couldn't be about me. The meeting ended with her offering me a summer position but not an invitation to return the next school year. As news spread, both employees and parents reached out to me in shock. Over the years, I kept replaying that day back in my head until it finally registered in my naïve brain. I was the only degreed African American employed there. Was my presence intimidating to her? I'll never have all the answers, but being a Black woman in America over the years has shown me life is not always fair. Being educated to top it off is a dangerous combination for some to handle.

After leaving her office, I went to my car and began crying uncontrollably. I felt defeated; I missed my family; and I was ready to go home, so that's what I did. Back to Louisville I went. I started a job teaching at a pretty new child care center where I found the ivory to my ebony. She is still one of the best friends I have today. I settled into a small house in the west end and focused on raising my baby girl, who was soon to be in middle school.

A few years after being back, I opened myself up to finding love again. Let's just say it was a whirlwind that I didn't foresee ending the way it did...but more about that later. When I got tired of crying over him, I decided I'd rather feel anything but sadness. Enter Mr. Red Flag himself. He's the one who almost broke me. No, he did break me. Though I was not blind to the fact that he was wrong for me, his affinity for being a dad always made me smile. So when 13 years after giving birth to my daughter I found myself positively pregnant again(after taking the third test just to make sure), I had no doubt we'd make great co-parents if nothing else.

I wasn't nervous about telling him, and I definitely wasn't prepared for his reaction. He didn't want another child, flat out, that's it. So what are you going to do about it? We continued to talk as if nothing had changed about our situation. Then it began:, the pushing me not to have the baby making subtle threats about his promised absence in the child's life. Day after day, he was one person in public and another when it came to me.

Anyone who knows me knows I am pro-choice, but personally abortion would not be mine. Until I found myself making a call to the clinic, he had won. He was happy; then the appointment came and went, and I was still pregnant. He was furious. The threats intensified. I had better not tell anyone it's his. Then magically, he no longer knew me; the baby wasn't his; we'd never been together. Poof he was gone.

I made my peace with it. I would never put myself in a position to be hurt this way again. Slowly I healed as the little one grew. When my son was born, my life again changed as it did with my daughter. They both saved me in different ways. I stopped having sex. At first I was just waiting until I found the right person, but it grew into a vow of celibacy. Was it hard, uh yeah. I'd be lying if I said it wasn't. Still the power of owning your decisions and having control and say over what you do or don't do with your body is indescribable. People who know, and have found out how long I've gone without sex (currently nine years) are baffled and sometimes give me a hard time about it. However, the freedom and peace I've achieved since making the choice cannot be matched.

Even though my chance at love prior to meeting Mr. Red Flag had ended abruptly, and by email mind you, with a clear mind I was able to think back on how things had unfolded and I still blush. I can vividly remember when I began to fall for him and how he made me feel safe, wanted, desired even. He was not a guy I would have typically fallen for but the conversation was engaging and intriguing. We couldn't take our eyes off of each other.

So the night I stood there waiting for him to kiss me, I got impatient and went in myself for it. I knew then that this feeling was possible, to once again love. This is why I haven't been able to settle. I want that spark. It's not always immediate, but there is a moment early on where things just click. The connection is made and you know it is something special. With this knowledge in mind I put thoughts of love and marriage on the backburner for the time to prepare for my newest addition.

I can recall my daughter's uneasiness upon hearing the news that her brother would be busting up our duo. I mean what was I thinking? We'd been just fine for 14 years before HE came! True to who she is though, she became his protector and best friend. Some Saturday mornings I could hear her whisper to him, "come on, let momma sleep," and then my door would close. There are so many words I could use to describe her but "thoughtful" always seems to resurface.

She's been consistently thoughtful over the years. I've always tried to shield her from the reality of just how hard life could be for us at times, but I'm sure she picked up on it. Proof of that came as she grocery shopped with my mom, and my mother relaying to me how sensible she was with money, often asking if the cost of items were too much. I often joke about how she sometimes forgets I'm the mom, but she truly has been my rock in times where all she should have been worried about was running around the playground.

I was so proud of the young lady she was becoming.

The years following my son's birth were pretty amazing. Navigating life with a newborn and a high schooler was an adventure all its own. I've made plenty of mistakes but those two are by far my greatest achievement. I worked on my little family, myself, my spiritual health and time moved along. Things were going well at work, and I was soon to have a high school graduate. I felt like I could conquer anything at this point. When my daughter left for school, I knew things would be different....I wasn't ready for just how different.

Here I am with a kid in pre-school and one in college. She had helped me more than I knew because this little person was now kicking my butt. I was tired all the time, and I missed my baby girl like crazy. Slowly I fell into a months' long depression that I still cannot completely put into words. I can remember being somewhat optimistic after a while thinking I was coming up for air. However, life was only at the start of what it had in store for me over the months to come.

There was disappointment, tragedy, loss, and an even deeper depression.

I disconnected from the world, the people who love me and went through the motions so much so I can't recall how I made it from point A to B many days. So I began to pray. I prayed when I didn't feel like it, when I felt I wasn't being heard, when nothing was changing, when I didn't even believe what I was saying I continued to pray. Then God sent two people, one who could tell something was going on, one who had no clue, and amazingly both lived far away. That's how he works, you know; he's kind of awesome like that.

As I began to share with my inner circle, some asked why I didn't reach out. At the time I couldn't put into words what I was feeling. I didn't know, so how could I tell you? But that's what we do: we slap bandages on and keep going without ever healing because we don't reach out; we don't get to the core of it all. So I'm telling you, keep pushing even when it hurts, when it's hard, when you see no results, but most of all talk to someone. God will give you the words, and, more importantly, he'll give you the right person to receive your words.

Finally, one night my son dropped some food on the floor and I went berserk. I ultimately realized my boy was only getting a shell of me, and now I was beginning to take things out on him. I saw a doctor, and began my road to true healing. It was a good thing I did, because my son was going to need me in a big way in the coming years. As my daughter was soaring toward her college degree, my baby boy was starting to ask questions about his father. I've always said it's not my story to tell but I have a smart kid which caused me to step up and reach out much sooner than I'd anticipated.

After blocking me on the social site I reached out to him on, I then found his phone number and texted his dad. He asked who I was, and when I "jogged" his memory, he said he would call him the next day. He didn't. God has a way of going before us and preparing the path you're headed toward. Thankfully my son was with my parents when I'd heard back from him and realized he wasn't going to step up. By the time I left work that day, the pain in my chest was unbearable, and my hands were shaking uncontrollably. I look at my boy now and all I can think is who in his right mind wouldn't want to know him — yet there we were.

I had to have a hard conversation with him so that healing could begin. Though my heart still aches for that particular absence he has in his life, that is in no way his fault, but he continues to question that. God covered me with a calmness and peace that only he could have. My son cried as I held him, asking why his dad didn't want to talk to him. I couldn't answer. I could only reassure him of my love.

We went on living the day to day but I could tell he was not OK. For a while, he had had anxieties about different things, but they were increasing, along with his anger. He worried way more than any child should. Most times I am able to talk him through his fears and help calm him. After a while, I recognized he needed more help than I could provide, and I wanted him to be able to cope even when I'm not around. I also realized his anxieties were heightening my own.

He began seeing a therapist. He was scared but very eager to go. He is making progress and likes to share his experience with others. There is nothing wrong with equipping our children with the tools they need to survive how crazy this world is fast becoming. I only hope we can begin to start normalizing therapy and mental health wellness.

FULL STOP!!!! Right here is when I began wrapping up what I wanted to say, and then life served a gut punch like I hadn't seen in my 41 years of living.

I could probably start a whole other project with what this part of 2020 would bring but let's just add it here.

A Freaking Pandemic

Before we left on spring break in March, I remember our boss calling us all together to talk about COVID-19. She mentioned the possibility of us not returning but at that time none of us realized the seriousness of this illness, including myself. I just kept thinking, "yeah, OK," then — boom! —state-wide shutdown. Talk about uncharted territory. Suddenly we found ourselves staying "safe at home." Maybe this time could be used to get things done that we'd been putting off. Or maybe we could just catch up on sleep, relax, and take advantage of the down time. Yeah, we're in a pandemic, a virus running rampant, but how many people did you actually know with it? Funny memes were flying; this would die down; and surely we'd be back to normal soon — right?

Nope. As our new reality began to set in, our annoyances with a situation that was out of our control did as well. I mean, please tell me how you explain to an extremely social and active 8-year-old that we will be spending now and the foreseeable future inside of our house?

And one who struggles with anxiety to boot! Whereas when I'd occasionally have a drink on the weekend after Mase was asleep, I was drinking nearly every day, earlier and heavier each day. Sure, I'd been a big-time drinker in college, but I had not put it away like that in years, yet here I was waking up with hangovers with a kid in the next room. We managed to make it through a spring break with no activities, a cancelled soccer season, virtual schooling, and were headed toward summer break. Big whoop, huh? Not like we can do anything...cue racism 2.0

A Voice Found Amid Riots

As the summer months raged on, I often wondered if America had really taken a look at why Colin did what he did, would we be experiencing what we are now. It was laughable to watch white people quoting Dr. King as if he was this beloved icon at the time he was leading the Civil Rights movement. Let me go back, though, I'm getting ahead of myself.

In February, Ahmaud Arbery had been killed running while black. It wasn't something the African American community hadn't seen before. Then in nearby Louisville, Kentucky, Breonna Taylor had been shot during the serving of a no-knock warrant in March. Again, an all-too-familiar scene we were unfortunately becoming numb to. Finally in May, George Floyd became the catalyst to an ire we could no longer push down. The media's go-to narrative that they had a past that warranted their deaths was not going to cut it this time. I'm sorry, since when did "guilty" equal a death sentence?

What the world was now witnessing was already long embedded in many of our minds. We were so drained as a people, literally checking in on each other, because the burden of watching brown bodies take their last breath at the hands of the police on camera was too much to bear anymore. I watched a clip recently where Dr. King said, “No longer are we going to allow police officers to beat us and trample over us and use horses and billy clubs on us in a corner. We’re gonna make it necessary for them to do it in the glaring light of public opinion.” How in 2020 was this sound bite still relevant? The response? Blue Lives Matter.

I have to break down the idiocy of that phrase. As an educator, if I saw someone harming a child, my first step is going to be to make sure the child is safe, then I'm going to call out the person doing harm. No ifs, ands, or buts. You were wrong and you need to face the consequences. I wouldn't for one minute think to say, "ohhhh we're not all like that." Of course we aren't but this one is, and that is what we are currently addressing. Yet instead of highlighting the problem at hand, we were being asked to celebrate the good police officers. Mind you a blue life is chosen and can be taken off and walked away from if you at any time feel disrespected, but I digress.

The outrage that what seemed like a large percentage of America felt however would soon go away. The blame once again was put on this preposterous idea of Black on Black crime being the REAL problem and the country would become even more divided.

Protests were taking place all across the country. My daughter, in the footsteps of her great-grandfather who had once marched with Dr. King for fair housing rights, was now front and center fighting for ironically some of the same things they had…some 50 years later. I joined her at one and I will never be able to put into words the array of feelings I had that day. As with any cause, you always have disagreements on how to push a message forward. Because of that, at times protests would later turn violent by not only those not truly dedicated to what we were trying to accomplish, but also those who intentionally wanted to undermine any progress that was being made. Did I agree with the violence? Let's just say America has a short memory of how many things have gotten done over the years in this country.

I remember watching a clip of comedian Michal Che where he said "As a country we can't even agree that Black lives matter. Not matter more, just matter and how Blacks were once fighting for Civil Rights not even equal rights and someone was still like, nah." It was so simple, hilarious, and sad at the same time. Yet this was our current reality. Soon all that was taking place began to spill over into friendships and families causing division among those you once loved and respected.

Already emotionally drained from what I was seeing, I began typing up a post on social media and gave no thought to how it would make me look or make others feel. After that day I just kept typing and losing “friends.” You know for some, the bottom line was as long as you’re not “acting Black” we’re OK with you. People were showing their true colors and to that I said: “Guess what? Black lives still matter.”

I will never go back to being silently Black. Naw, I'm UNAPOLOGETICALLY BLACK, my friends. My daughter texted me one day and said, "every time I get an alert, it's you going off. You need to log off"...still I couldn't. My friend mentioned her mom being afraid of possible backlash and she told her, "no, Kay has found her voice; let her talk."

Those you'd always had suspicions about began confirming their racist views through the things they were posting, and others by their eerie silence. I had a few white friends I was close enough to that I felt comfortable speaking about my feelings. I had knots in my stomach when I met up with them on the walking track that day but I did it. Both admitted they didn't know what to say/post, afraid it might be the wrong thing. This, however, I explained was not the time to be scared. Allies were needed and your true allies quickly made themselves known. Some you expected and others were a pleasant surprise. On the other side, you had those who were not trying to understand anything they'd never experienced for themselves. The extreme opposite of that end were the ones who felt overly guilty for whatever reason and then began looking to you to help them through their realizations that, yeah, racism is actually still a thing even though we'd had a Black family in the White House. Like, are you kidding me?!

I think the worst of it came when as I mentioned earlier white folk were quoting MLK urging for peace, and posting clips of Black "spokespersons" saying things that made them feel good about their jacked-up feelings. We were not here to make you comfortable and neither was he, which is why there were constant threats to his life. You don't get to tell us how to stand up for rights we shouldn't be fighting for in the first place. Yet whitesplaining was at an all-time high. How in the world do you dismiss what someone is feeling? Someone's personal experience? As if you know better?

Years of letting shit go had taken its toll, and I was done biting my tongue. The subtleties of racism were becoming more blatant, deliberate. Biases that, though we all have them in some ways, were becoming what seemed to be a cop-out in a time with so much access to information. We were being pushed past the point of making sure to watch your Black girl tone and working three times as hard to make sure you were taken seriously. Now people were finding out who I am as a whole and what has shaped me.

We had dared to share the experience that was ours only to be told....ok BUT. Or worse than that complete silence from those we trusted and believed that when it came down to it could be our voice when others refused to hear ours. Right now, right here, in this moment I need you to just listen and hear me. Then before I could process my ongoing transformation it was time to head back to work, where, yes, African Americans are represented, but in low numbers.

I was friends with many of my white co-workers on social media and had been shouting my truth as loud as I could; now I was going back to work alongside them. Every instance of racism I'd experienced while on the job kept coming to mind. Some stood out more than others. Allow me to share a few:

- After Obama was re-elected I had walked by and heard some co-workers talking about him being in office. I could not believe the things I was hearing. I knew their circumstances; they benefitted from many of the programs the Democratic Party backed, so why exactly do you have a problem with this Democrat president? Talk about voting against your own best interests. I never made it known that I'd overheard them, just made a mental note of who'd been a part of that conversation.

- Both a co-teacher and a manager had at separate times said the N-word to me while conveying information about a situation with one of our students. While I was able to tell my co-teacher, "hey, that's not OK; don't do it again," I couldn't muster up the courage to say it to one of my "bosses." I just stood there wide eyed not believing she thought it was OK, even if she was repeating what a parent had said.

- When I took on the role of supervisor, I had to work with other department heads in some capacity. There was one particular woman who consistently had to double check and verify information I would give her. Sometimes she wouldn't even wait until I was out of earshot to ask someone else without brown skin the same question and many times that person fell under my supervision.
- I was so excited to wear a pair of earrings my mom bought me that

said "Black Excellence." When a fellow teacher saw them, she said, "We get it, Kezia, you're Black!" She was joking, this I knew, but I was getting to a point that I could find no humor in someone laughing about me celebrating who I was.

- Later that same day, a former supervisor asked me why it was OK for me to wear them. She stated how she felt like if she wore some celebrating her heritage she'd be looked at badly. I had to explain that we celebrate our skin color because no one else does, how she'd always seen herself represented in the media and beyond, so why would she even want to wear some?

That first day back, my desire to maintain professionalism because you don't have the luxury of being labeled the angry Black woman in the workplace was quickly becoming a non-factor. Yet in my head I kept hearing: "You are the minority here, Kay. You are in a leadership position now...tread light, tread light.. As soon as I walked in, one of the teachers gave me a pin that read "Slap your local racist." From then on, whether they loved me, or silently hated me, I no longer had any qualms about being my true authentic self. I tried to settle back into my work routine but was quickly reminded that, yeah, race relations are boiling over but we're also still in the midst of a pandemic…a freaking pandemic.

Rona, is that you?

Months went by, and masks and social distancing became the norm, but not everyone was taking it seriously. Even as numbers began climbing, you still questioned whether it would actually make it to your doorstep. The implications of the virus, while not physically having it, began to take over your mind as we began to understand, "hey, this thing is not going away."

My true breaking point (or so I thought at the time) began on a Friday morning in September when I got a message from my dad. I was sitting in a meeting at work when it popped up on my phone that he needed to talk to my brothers and me about something. This did not sit right with me at all. Let me give you a little background. My dad beat prostate cancer years ago, but guess how I found out he may have had it? With the congregation at our church when he announced it from the pulpit. He is very casual in his delivery of things even when it is serious. We had almost lost him in a car accident as well a few years earlier, so to say I was freaking out is an understatement.

So I excused myself and went to call him. He of course tried to assure me everything was OK before finally telling me his kidneys were beginning to fail and it was time to start dialysis. Ummmm, OK Dad, no biggie. My friend happened to hear me talking in the hallway and came out just as the tears started welling up in my eyes. She hugged me, I took a breath and headed back into my meeting. It wasn't until my boss repeated my name for a response to something she'd just said that

I realized I had completely zoned out. I told her I had to leave and walked out, followed by another friend who was there with me. I told her what was going on and quickly left. By that evening I had calmed down considerably after talking to my mom and brothers about how we'd be moving forward.

The next morning, my son had soccer practice, so my focus was on him. Due to miscommunication of the start time we got there just as his team was finishing up. He, of course, lost it and began crying non- stop. I was in the front seat taking deep breaths trying to calm him, squeezing the steering wheel tighter and tighter and then the tears started to fall. I'm not sure how long I sat in that parking lot but eventually I pulled it together and we went on about our day.

By Sunday, I had pushed through and felt OK. Then Monday night I was texting with my circle of sisters. We were going back and forth about something, I can't even remember what, when the conversation took a turn. I got so angry and then extremely sad, and I knew immediately that it was me because any other day I would have brushed off what had been said. I got in the car and drove to my mom's house and told her I needed help. Not tomorrow, not later, today…right now. A good friend from church was able to connect me to a therapist so that I could begin the process of healing from so many things I'd had no idea had been affecting me. I was putting in the work, pandemic still raging, people still dying, racism still boiling over, and then….

12/1/20—I'm struggling y'all. This is different from my seasonal depression spells. I genuinely hate the world we're living in. I love to laugh and excuse my language but shit's just not funny anymore. I've had hard times in my life and hope is something I've NEVER lost, but it is running extremely thin. I didn't view the world like this when 2020 began. While I'm grateful for my eyes being opened to so many things this year, I can't stand the view many days. I'm angry and I don't want to be but it constantly swells for a myriad of reasons. I know God owes me nothing and doesn't have to do another thing for me because he's already blessed me immensely. Still I question what did I do so wrong to have to struggle in some of the ways I do even when I know he doesn't operate that way. I'm tired y'all, in a way I've never been before. No, I don't want to hurt myself, so don't worry about that but I'm just...just an unexplainable tired. People love to say your breakthrough is right around the corner when Satan starts to attack, but hell mine has been around the corner for a few too many years now. I mean how wide and long is this corner folk are talking about?! Why am I sharing? I'm never one to shy away from transparency so here I am asking for the prayers of the righteous in this moment. I know there are others who will read this and feel the same and I want them to know we are not alone even when it feels like we are. Please don't call me even though I know some of y'all will, just know I won't be answering right now, lol. I need prayer, that's it. Love y'all.

12/27/20—And then there was COVID. 2020 couldn't just leave quietly. Prayers for our household. I think I'm more scared of the young human I'll be quarantined with than the actual virus.

12/28—It is going to be an adjustment living apart in the same house but I'd hate to give this to my boy. He teared up yesterday and said he can't go 10 days without hugs and kisses. Later he asked if I was gonna die. You know usually you can say with some confidence no it's just a cold. But as I said "no," I couldn't help but think how this thing is taking African Americans on away from here in numbers. Which is what many of you must have realized as you called to check on me. A worry that hadn't been there began to rush over me, then Mason asked me: "How are you so calm with something that's not calm?" And I immediately knew how:

God's grace, mercy and peace that passes all understanding. He had already gone before me to prepare my mind. He's got me.

12/29/20—Hey friends! After a tough day yesterday, I woke up feeling a bit better this morning, just severely fatigued. Went on about my day then realized I couldn't smell. My son came and got me because the cat had just peed on the brand new rug my daughter gave me for Christmas. I was livid, mad the whole time I was cleaning. Then it hit me, this should stink to high heaven, but it didn't. I practically put my nose down into rug, still nothing. So I started smelling everything around the house until I thought, "OK, maybe I should stop inhaling so many toxic things." It was gone. Got over that trauma, then lost my sense of taste a few hours later. Mase is being a real sport; we just take turns freaking out. Thinking this may be a good time to start eating vegetables since I can't taste them anyway. Thank y'all for EVERYTHING!

12/30/20—Felt pretty awful this morning. I believe by the afternoon I was feeling better, but the emotional toll had set in and I rarely left the bed. During the day I found a movie my phone had put together of our trip to Kings Island Winter Fest last year. I sent it to Mason and after watching it he came in crying. He said he wasn't sad that he just really liked it. He later told me he'd made a decision that we should get the vaccine so things can go back to normal, and we can do things together again.

12/31/20—Y'all, Kirsten just dropped some stuff off for me. The doorbell rang and by the time I got to the door, all I saw was smoke from her tires peeling out. Her test came back negative so I guess she's not taking any chances

12/31/20—Food now tastes like a mixture of dirt and chalk. Yes I've tasted both, I work with littles.

12/31/20—Was looking through my memories and noticed I haven't really made any resolutions for a while. This year will be no different. Was trying to think of what I wanted to say to sum things up. It practically wrote itself. I'm literally going into 2021 with COVID. We kid but surely Ashton and his huge camera crew will be jumping out at midnight to let us know we'd been punked. No words 'cause I currently can't even stop laughing at how ridiculous my life currently is...but I'm alive, thank you Lord.

1/3/21—Still no smell, but taste is kind of coming back. Symptoms not as bad today. Just ridiculously tired. Rest is the only thing that helps, COVID does not give you ANY choice in the matter. Pretty sure I'm delirious. I'm currently trying to figure out how I can sleep in my boots without putting my feet on the bed. Thank you, Jermelle, for letting me get out my crazy thoughts everyday...you better delete

EVERY text. Dee for continuing to check in even though I didn't always respond. There are way too many to name, so please don't be upset with me. But can't forget about my 2 nurses as my daughter calls them, my mom and Mase. Y'all have truly lifted me up and pulled me through. Just wanted to check in before I check out. God has some things he needs me to do so I'm banning myself from pastimes that don't allow me to do it. I pray this year brings you all healing, peace, new outlooks, prosperity beyond your wildest dreams, and crazy fun adventures.

1/6/20—Prayers y'allllll! Been in contact with Mason's school nurse since last week. She had cleared him to go back today since we've been isolated from one another (it's really been hard for him). Our quarantine ended yesterday, but I got him tested just to be sure. He's positive, and she said even though he's been in quarantine and has had no symptoms, regulations now say he has to start his quarantine over again. He just stopped crying. This thing messes with you in too many ways.

1/6/20—Had a pretty bad breakdown a little earlier. I'm so loved and supported and look to God for guidance but am feeling so helpless, overwhelmed, and just plain lonely. Mase and I hugged for so long after he found out; we hadn't touched for 10 days before that. I just keep thinking of the time wasted when all he needed was a touch from me and I was being cautious, yet still he got it. Then I think of those in the hospital who were never allowed to see or touch their family before succumbing to this horrible virus. So I begin to thank God that I am recovering. Then fatigue sets in again, and you can't keep a coherent thought. I remember on my worst day asking God to please not let me die;, I'm not ready to go. How sobering is it to pray that prayer with a sincere heart because you've watched this thing take people one by one?? I remember another time when Mase thought he was getting a symptom and I reached out to hold his hand and he backed away from me. And though I absolutely understood his fear, my heart broke. So now you worry about how others will accept you once you're better. I just want to lie on my mom and hug my dad but can't right now, and that is a hurting feeling. In all that I keep coming back to wondering how people are surviving who don't have the solid rock to stand on. If you don't have God in your life, I implore you to search your heart for him because he is there waiting for you. Thanks for the prayers and encouragement, y'all. Writing helps me to get these feelings out so thanks for reading my posts.

1/9/21—Cards and care packages started showing up today. If y'all could have seen the spark in his eyes and that goofy smile. He was beyond excited to let me know he'd received more mail than I did today. I don't even know what to say: this little boy has some village. We are extremely blessed. I was just talking to my mom about how this has really been a lesson and challenge for me in letting others help. We talked about how we deny others the chance to be blessed by blessing us, and I am so guilty of that always trying to do everything myself. Yet God has created a space for me to allow others to serve, which is a very humbling and amazing experience.

1/12/21—I prayed last night that today would be better physically. You see, yesterday I spent the majority of my day in the bed because I was so dizzy. It seemed as though I was feeling really good so I got fully dressed, like actually put a bra on in I don't know how long. I headed to the couch to take my daily meds while I was talking to my daughter on the phone. Then out of nowhere I told her I had to hang up because I'd started to feel nauseous. At that point I was frozen with pain as well and called out to Mase to bring me some crackers. Feeling like I had a grip on things, I headed to the bathroom and realized my smell was coming back with a bang and everything STUNK! I made it to my room to lie down and then felt it rise again. I stood up, walked a few feet, and out it came. Mase yelled out, "are you OK, Mom?"

"No," I said in almost a whisper.

He came in, threw a towel on the throw up, and said, "go to the bathroom" before storming off. Yeah, he was over me at that point. After that, things were up and down and then I read about a young lady who had attended my alma mater passing from COVID. I couldn't deal. Why were young healthy people dying? Why were people seemingly recovering and then dying? The tears began to fall and for a second time since getting the Corona virus I found myself pleading with God to let me live. I just kept saying "my babies" over and over. I can't leave them. I don't want to die like this, not yet, I have things to do. You get to the point where even though you're starting to feel better you wonder what could happen if you close your eyes and go to sleep. I hit the shower, the best doctor I've ever met. When I got out, my mom had called. She called again and we talked. I didn't tell her the thoughts I'd been having, but the more I could hear her voice the calmer I became. Eventually I fell asleep only to wake up several times crying, in constant fear that I wouldn't see the next day...but I did. Another day I'd made it, living with COVID.

1/14/21—I want nothing more than to go stay with my parents when our quarantine is up tomorrow but I can't bring myself to do it. If there's the slightest chance that I could still pass it to them, I'd be devastated. I just miss them.

1/28—I was halfway through my day when it hit me I'd been feeling good all morning. I continued on scared to claim it for fear I'd jinx things. 7:30 came and I began sending texts to my family and close friends rejoicing that I believed I was on my way out of this thing finally. Then dread hit me as I prepared for bed. I hated the grip it could cause on your mind. I kept thinking, "will this be what they say after I pass? 'She had just texted," she was feeling better, "we don't know what happened.'" I prayed mightily as I laid my head down and as hard as it was, I drifted off to sleep. I woke several times at which time I thanked God that I was still here. The next morning I just began to worship God for so many reasons. He had shown me so many things through songs placed on my heart and mind. I had too much left to do in this world. God had begun a work in me and it was not yet completed. Now here I am, 10 almost 11 months after the world had gone crazy and fallen apart, 33 days after COVID had invaded my mind and body, completing my first assignment of many more, my story.

Life after COVID, 2020, and all the Crap in Between

To keep from going insane my motto became this, which I posted on 1/7/21:"It is OK to NOT agree to disagree. Some things are just fundamentally wrong and if you don't get that, you are most certainly the problem. You can also condemn something without giving examples of why something else was similarly wrong." What prompted that, you ask? Racism, for me at least had sneakily made its way into politics, which normally I wouldn't touch with a 10-foot pole. Being that I could no longer stay silent about much of anything,

I found myself going back and forth with people following the Capitol insurrection all while trying to recover from COVID, ultimately writing these words on 1/21/21: "Looooong post that may be jumbly in nature! I keep seeing people trying to 'keep the peace' with their posts in the post-election days. I get it, I did it for far too long. However, at a certain point no matter how hard something is to learn, see, and digest, you cannot unsee it after your eyes have been opened. I've said it before, it is OK to NOT agree to disagree. Politics aside, for me there is a huge difference between Republicans and 'Trump Supporters.' A conversation with one may get heated but you can still listen and see where they are coming from. The other would be an incoherent mess. I do realize this may take out a few more of my Fb 'friends,' but I won't sit silently by anymore while you attempt to justify a vote you proudly gave to a racist...and he IS that, plain and simple. I'm not even touching all the other questionable crap he said and did over the last four years, 'just' the RACIST parts. We are not to judge one another so I won't, that is for God and God alone to do, so let's just stick with facts. Many of Trump's followers have admitted to being empowered by his words and that made America a very dangerous place for Black and brown people during his presidency. I've watched people with sincerity tout Donald Trump as a man of God as to why they supported him. Umm, what doctrine are you studying and where do you attend church so I can stay far away. You want to be honest? There are a very large number of conservative Democrats, yet most of us realize it is not our place, or at least shouldn't be to make decisions about our fellow man's life. I want to help make your life better, not tell you what's wrong with it then walk away. Being a 'Trump Republican' is not synonymous with being a Christian; you don't have that market cornered. You are not a victim, and NO I do not feel the least bit sorry that your privilege has gone unchecked for so long that you really feel attacked by the truly disenfranchised. Sorry, but I'll save my tears for the mother who was guilted into having a baby she wasn't ready for, then could never get herself together for, and her child who will later be criticized for not being able to break family curses. I'll save them for the person who committed suicide instead of never coming out because of what we Christians yelled at them their entire lives. For the child who now hates America because their family dared to ask for a chance at a better life and instead we separated them and gave them a nice cold floor and cage to stay in. Many came to worship a man, a slogan, a MAGA flag and that is not what God called us to do. Racism is NOT a difference of opinion. It is what

Trump believes is ok, and your vote said it was ok too. We are not the same."

After that I decided to give social media a true break because now I had a message to finish, but not without some parting words: I want to talk a little about transparency today. God did not bring you through some of the things you've survived for you to keep it to yourself. So many times we suffer in silence, and that shouldn't be the norm. I haven't always been as outspoken as I am now publicly or with people I'm not close to, but I'm telling you, your story could change or even save someone's life. My pastor has a saying that confession is good for the soul but not always good for your reputation. That's why you have to be prayerful and led before speaking. When I tested positive for COVIDI didn't think twice about sharing. I wanted all the prayers I could get, prayers specifically for what I was going through! Slowly my inbox filled with those that had gone through it, or were going through it. I was stunned. There are still so many unknowns about this thing and I know it can feel taboo to have had or have it. However, if you've endured it you know how frightening it can be. I'm in support groups but being able to talk to people you know and trust about it is beyond comforting. I am basically symptom free but am now struggling mentally with the fact that many people seemingly recover then out of nowhere they are gone. I lost count of how many times I woke up crying one night because I feared not only leaving this Earth but also that my son would have to be the one to find me. I am a believer, yes, but I am human as well, and those thoughts can overtake you sometimes. There is way too much going on in this world currently to not keep things all the way real with each other. You love someone? Tell them. You miss someone? Call them. Someone annoy the heck out of you??? Tell them that, too...just lovingly, lol. As always, thanks for listening, love y'all. Let's stay prayed up and CONNECTED!

I see my therapist regularly so that watching people lose their battle with COVID so often now doesn't take me back to a dark place especially people my age and younger who were fine just a few months ago. Even as I sit here finishing up,

I have to be honest about my current progress. Some days are good. Others I'm still figuring out how to live a productive life with what is now the new normal for my body. If nothing else, I can no longer just say listen to your body, because it makes the decisions for me. How does that look? Plans may have to be pushed, changed, or cancelled. Sometimes it's going to bed for the night as soon as I get home each day. Sometimes it's using mouthwash and popping in some gum until later because if I brush my teeth before seven a.m. I'm going to spend the next 15minutes throwing up. It also means continuing to have groceries delivered or picked up because as I learned the hard way you may find yourself doubled over the cart gasping for air after only running in for a few things. God definitely put my friend there that day to help me finish bagging and get out to my car. Yet if these adjustments help me see another day to do the work God has for me, then that's what has to happen for now...maybe forever. We just still don't know enough about this thing.

So why have I chosen to share my story with you? Because on the outside looking in most would assume I have it all together. Master's in Public Administration, bachelor's in Child Development and Family Relations, minor in Music, supervisor on my job, great family and friends, mom of a college graduate now teacher, and a super talented and witty boy, preacher's daughter, nice car, nice home. Writing it out I'm impressed myself.

Still it is a struggle to even get out of bed sometimes. I get lonely even with people around, I get sad, I question why I don't have a significant other, and there are times I have more bills than money. Am I where I want to be in life? No, but I'm happy at this point in my journey and I don't want to miss out on my daily blessings hoping for bigger ones that may or may not ever come. Life is good, but it's also hard. We need to be more transparent about that fact and help each other through. I heard a preacher once say we're all going through different seasons. We need to remember the one we just came out of and recognize when someone is going through it to be of encouragement to them.

I had something to say, and if you get nothing else from these pages just know you're not alone. Take life one day, one hour, heck one minute at a time if you need to. Start over as many times as you have to, just don't stop trying, don't stop hoping, don't stop dreaming, and don't stop pushing. If no one else has told you today, I love you, and I'm rooting for you.

"Life is amazing. And then it's awful. And then it's amazing again. And in between the amazing and awful it's ordinary and mundane and routine. Breathe in the amazing, hold on through the awful, and relax and exhale during the ordinary. That's just living heartbreaking, soul healing, amazing, awful, ordinary life. And it's breathtakingly beautiful." L. R. Knost

www.ingramcontent.com/pod-product-compliance
Lightning Source LLC
LaVergne TN
LVHW010105110826
845155LV00028B/483